Table of Contents

I0448719

Abstract

The prosperity of a nation is directly linked to the education of its population. An educated population has the knowledge base and skill necessary to translate its country's natural wealth (people, land, resources) into material wealth (economic strength and competitiveness). In Nigeria, this link is missing, undermined by rampant corruption at all levels of its educational system. The most damaging aspect of corruption is the amount of money lost through practices such as embezzlement. To prevent such losses, this paper recommends that the Government of Nigeria undertake a comprehensive anti-corruption campaign centered around establishing accountability throughout its educational sector. The analysis suggests that accountability is best achieved through *indirect* methods aimed at increasing capacity in three distinct, yet overlapping areas: data collection, management, and oversight. Those who oppose this approach argue the most effective means of battling corruption is through direct measures that use punitive acts as deterrents against further corruption. The paper concludes with specific recommendations that could help the Nigerian Government reduce the impacts of corruption in its school system and achieve its objective of universal, free, and compulsory education for its youth.

I. Introduction

The date was September 8, 2009, a Tuesday not unlike any other. The President of the United States could have been anywhere from Washington to Tokyo and all points in between. Yet, on this day, President Obama's destination was Wakefield High School in Arlington, Virginia. In a historic, nationally televised address to America's youth, the President's message was simple: The future prosperity of the country is directly related to the education of its youth. In unequivocal terms, he told America's youth, "If you quit on school—you're not just quitting on yourself, you're quitting on your country".[1]

Understanding this fundamental truth, the United Nations introduced its "Education For All" (EFA) movement in 1990.[2] Ten years later at the World Education Forum, Nigeria was one of 164 nations that pledged to achieve EFA goals by 2015 and introduced its Universal Basic Education (UBE) program as a strategy to meet these commitments.[3] Unfortunately, Nigeria's efforts to improve its educational system have proven largely ineffective, plagued by rampant corruption at each level of government.

While corrupt practices in Nigeria's educational sector manifest themselves in many ways, the most damaging aspect of corruption is the amount of money lost through practices such as embezzlement. In fact, research shows, as much as 80 percent of funds allocated for education do not make it to the intended programs.[4] To prevent such losses, the Government of Nigeria (GoN) should undertake a comprehensive anti-corruption campaign centered around establishing accountability throughout its educational sector. This strategy achieves accountability through *indirect* methods aimed at increasing capacity in three distinct, yet overlapping areas: data collection, management, and oversight.

The potential benefits of such an approach are immense. In the short-term, it would allow the GoN to achieve its policy objective of universal, free, and compulsory education for its youth.[5] In the long-term, it would encourage foreign investment, reduce the influence of extremist groups such as Boko Haram, and enhance Nigeria's prospects for economic growth and competitiveness. The greatest benefit, however, is that such a program would invest in Nigeria's most precious resource: the minds of its 168 million people.

II. Background

The Importance of Education

Addressing the role of education in society, the Swiss developmental psychologist Jean Piaget once said, "The principle goal of education is to create men who are capable of doing new things, not simply of repeating what other generations have done – men who are creative, inventive and discoverers."[6] In other words, education is more than simply the procurement of knowledge for the benefit of the individual. It's an investment in the future of society, a means to allow for the continual growth and evolution of the *collective*.

An educated society is one that can think for itself. Education generates *ideas*. In this, its real power lies. Without education, new and creative ideas are in short supply, and the ceiling for societal growth is extremely limited. Worse, an uneducated population is extremely vulnerable to manipulation. Unable to generate ideas for themselves, they unwittingly grasp onto ideas that are propagated by others. Ideas that are destructive to society, advanced by groups like Nigeria's Islamic militant organization Boko Haram, whose goal is the acquisition of power and control.[7] In summary, education forms the critical link between a country's natural wealth (people, land, resources) and its material wealth (economic strength and global competitiveness). In parts of the world where this link is missing, extensive poverty, high unemployment, and instability often result.

III. Main Body

The Objective

The objective provides purpose to planning and answers the question "to what end?"[8] About the importance of the objective, the great Prussian military theorist Carl von Clausewitz famously said, "Pursue one great decisive aim with force and determination—a maxim which should take first place among all causes of victory."[9] Clausewitz's truism, while applicable at all levels of war, is especially true during the military planning process. Planners must always remain cognizant of the objective, lest the entire effort becomes pointless.[10] Additionally, the evaluation of the objective should be an iterative process, always ensuring the stated ends are achievable given current means and constraints.[11] Looking at Nigeria's educational system, the policy objective is clear: "Ensure that by 2015 all children have access to, and complete, free and compulsory primary education of good quality."[12] The following paragraphs seek to discover the root

3

causes that prevent Nigeria from achieving this objective, and suggest an approach that allows for a reversal of this trend.

The Problem – The Nigerian Paradox

Nigeria is not fulfilling the commitments it made to Education For All in 2000.[13] As Otive Igbuzor confirms, "If current trends continue, the target of achieving universal primary education by 2015 will be missed by at least a decade."[14] Today, an estimated ten million (of thirty million) Nigerian school-aged children are not in school;[15] the country's literacy rate is estimated at 61 percent;[16] and 50 percent of the nation's primary school teachers are unqualified.[17] Accordingly, this failure to properly educate the nation's youth has had devastating impacts on Nigeria's economic growth and prosperity. Unemployment is at 21 percent and rising;[18] the percentage of the population living below the poverty line is at 70 percent;[19] and Nigeria's misery index, which combines unemployment and inflation, is at 36 percent.[20] All of these metrics place Nigeria near the bottom of the world rankings. Given the country's immense human and natural resources, it's an equation that does not add up. Fittingly, the situation has been termed "The Nigerian Paradox".[21]

For answers to this paradox, the Swiss Agency for Development and Cooperation (SDC) offers some insight. It contends, "The fact that too many developing countries are in dire economic straits today—even those with ample natural resources—is strongly linked to the susceptibility to *corruption* of the ruling class."[22] Such is the case in Nigeria, where corruption is so intertwined with society that it is viewed as a normal aspect of everyday life.[23] Indeed, in its 2011 world rankings, Transparency International ranked Nigeria among the most corrupt nations in the world, giving it a "highly corrupt" 2.4 score.[24] Understanding the symbiotic nature of corruption to Nigerian society is critical when formulating an anti-corruption strategy and will be discussed in-depth later in this analysis.

The effects of corruption, while damaging enough to society writ large, have had a crippling effect on the nation's educational system, which is already beset by an acute shortage of qualified teachers, adequate infrastructure, and available instructional material. Corruption exacerbates these problems by robbing the system of the funding designed to fix these shortcomings in the first place. As Emmanuel Ejere states, "It is obvious that not all funds allocated for the UBE program are used for the intended purposes, due to high level of corruption in key implementing agencies and wasteful spending."[25] The resultant lack of funding manifests itself in the form of dilapidated schools. For example, studies show that 12 percent of students sit on the floor, 38 percent of classrooms have no ceilings, 87 percent of classrooms are overcrowded, and 77 percent of students lack textbooks.[26] Given these conditions, it is clearly not possible to achieve *universal* basic education, let alone make it *compulsory*. So despite laudable political commitments to education for all and a sound program (UBE) to meet these commitments, the entire effort is undermined and made worse by corruption. Thus, a nation with immense natural resources routinely ranks among the poorest nations in the world.

The Environment – The Problem in Context

Having defined the problem, it's important to put it into proper context before moving forward with a solution. Looking at the current environmental conditions in Nigeria, two major issues come to the forefront. First, because of its historical roots, Nigerians view corruption as an integral part of everyday life. Second, corruption continues to thrive because the system allows it. Together, these factors both inform and constrain possible solution-sets.

Corruption has been a part of Nigerian society since the colonial days of the early 20th Century. However, the early days of independence in the 1960s saw the full transformation of corruption into its definitive (and current) form. With the anti-colonial ideology that once unified the country long gone, politicians unabashedly used corruption as a means for maintaining power. Martin Meredith, in his epic novel *The Fate of Africa*, captures the essence of this transformation: "In Nigeria, the first years of independence became an orgy of power being turned into profit. Power itself in effect came to rest on the ability to bribe."[27]

It was a situation for which Nigeria had no defense. Lacking the institutional capacity and educated population base to thwart these changes, Nigeria was laid bare, at the mercy of those motivated only by greed and lust for power. As this condition was allowed to fester and grow, corruption became woven into the very fabric of society. Nigerians came to view it as normal way of life, accepted as a means of getting by, earning a living, obtaining a service or avoiding hassle.[28] Consequently, Nigerians today simply don't view themselves as corrupt and meet attempts to highlight corruption as a problem of their society with extreme sensitivity.[29] It is exactly this mentality that makes devising solutions so difficult.

Additionally, corruption thrives because the system makes it both easy and profitable.[30] This should come as little surprise considering those responsible for building the system are the same people who benefit most from corrupt practices. Therefore, when seeking strategies that will fundamentally alter the system, planners must bear in mind they are working not only against history, but also working against a system that is designed to allow corruption from the very highest levels.

Taken as a whole, the above analysis offers useful insights into the viability of possible solutions. Specifically, overreliance on direct attacks on corruption, while having an understandable appeal, are likely to be ineffective given the inherent sensitivities of the population and the deeply imbedded nature of the problem. Therefore, strategies must be devised that can attack corruption through *indirect* methods. As Shah and Schacter state, "the key lies in finding alternative 'entry points' that will lead inevitably to the underlying governance-based drivers of corruption."[31] Increasing accountability is one such entry point. Therefore, this analysis offers the following course of action: the Government of Nigeria should undertake a comprehensive anti-corruption campaign centered around establishing accountability throughout its educational sector. Free of the burden of corruption, Nigeria can reconstitute its school system and achieve its objective of universal, free, and compulsory education for all its youth.

The Solution – Incentivizing Accountability

Merriam-Webster defines accountability as "an obligation or willingness to accept responsibility or to account for one's actions."[32] In the educational sector, accountability extends from the political leadership all the way down to the classroom level. The idea of accountability is important because those who hold themselves accountable are more likely to conduct business in an open, honest manner consistent with accepted societal norms. In Nigeria, leaders are not accountable because the system lacks the capacity to hold them accountable. Laws and controls meant to limit corrupt practices may be in place, but these measures are meaningless if the system lacks the means to enforce them. With limited risk of being discovered, there is little incentive for leaders to be accountable. Therefore, the recommended approach aims to *incentivize accountability* by increasing capacity in three distinct, yet overlapping areas: data collection, management, and oversight.

Improving Data Collection

Corruption thrives as a result of a *lack of data*. Without data, an "information asymmetry" is created between officials and the general public.[33] The entire system becomes shrouded in ambiguity and the general public must *assume* that public funds are being used wisely and for intended purposes. As evidenced by the multi-million-dollar corruption scandal that rocked Long Island's Roslyn School District in 2004, this situation is extremely vulnerable to corruption.[34] Leaders realize the information required to hold them accountable is absent, and

8

thus have no qualms about partaking in corrupt practices. Therefore, the goal of increasing the data collection capacity of the system is to empower key stakeholders with knowledge to make informed decisions. As stated in the 2010 Nigeria Education Data Survey (NEDS), "Over the years, a major challenge faced by policy makers in Nigeria is obtaining reliable information to enhance the decision-making process."[35] The presence of data does this by increasing the transparency in the system and allowing informed planning to occur.

Whereas a lack of data shrouds a system in ambiguity, the presence of accurate, reliable data allows it to operate transparently vis-à-vis the operators and the general public. Jacques Hallak and Muriel Poisson, in their book *Corrupt schools, corrupt universities: What can be done?*, define transparency in education as "the extent to which stakeholders can understand the basis on which educational resources are allocated to their individual establishment and how they are used."[36] In other words, a transparent process is one that is visible, predictable, and understandable to an outside audience.[37] The relationship between transparency and accountability is direct and inseparable, and incentivizes accountability in two ways.[38] First, as a deterrent, transparency makes people less likely to act unethically because they know their actions are observable. Second, as an enabler, transparency enforces accountability by making people more aware of how processes are completed. Free from the information asymmetry that leads to assumptions and inaction, people are empowered to take ownership of their programs.[39] In a democratic state like Nigeria, effective ownership manifests itself as political pressure on the country's leadership to make the necessary changes to the program. Hallak and Poisson capture the essence of this strategy as such: "Transparency enables institutions—and the public—to make informed political decisions, it improves the accountability of governments, and reduces the scope for corruption."[40]

The second benefit of increasing the data collection capacity of Nigeria's educational system is it allows informed planning to take place. As Ejere states, "Without accurate and reliable data, no meaningful planning can be done and it will be difficult to avoid policy breakdown at the implementation stage."[41] Specifically, in the context of balancing ends, ways, and means, the presence of data allows for the measurement of the means available to the planner. This measurement is critical to the establishment of reference points and milestones in the planning process. Reference points provide planners with a known starting point from which they can measure deviations as new data becomes available. For example, if a strategy calls for 100 desks to go to school A, but the planner has no idea how many desks currently reside in the system, it's impossible to move forward with any kind of fidelity in planning and execution.

Milestones, which form key decision points along the path towards the desired endstate, are the basis from which to measure planning and policy implementation progress. Data is instrumental in this process in that it provides the means to measure whether or not certain milestones have been achieved. Accountability is a natural extension of this ability because officials realize that the system now has the capacity to hold them accountable. Using the example from above, if the plan calls for 100 desks to be provided to school A, but school

A only receives 75 desks, there exists a clear basis for questioning or investigation. Empowered both with knowledge (through transparency) and a means to hold officials accountable, key stakeholders can make informed decisions as how to best influence future policy implementation.

Strengthening Management Capacity

Managers implement policy. They provide the critical connection between policy directives and policy results. Managers of an educational system require a diverse skill-set, ranging anywhere from planning to accounting. In planning, managers must be able to capture the data, compare the data to existing plans, and based on that comparison, make decisions on the future direction of the program. The development of effective long-term plans avoids the pitfalls of the compulsory use of funds (short-term projects designed to use up the budget) that only facilitates corrupt practices.[42] In accounting, managers are entrusted to ensure allocated resources are spent in ways consistent with policy objectives.[43] Failures of management offer innumerable avenues for corruption to occur. As Hallak and Poisson state, "Improving skills in management, accounting, monitoring, and audit are basic requirements for reducing corruption in education."[44] Therefore, for countries that lack sufficient capacity for effective management, this area quickly becomes a focal point for any anti-corruption strategy.

In Nigeria, the educational system suffers from a critical shortage of qualified managers. The situation is especially acute in the areas of accounting and

11

finance, where the government sorely needs the addition of qualified accountants, auditors, and statisticians. In lack of this skill-set, the most of the important aspects of the budgeting and accounting duties are left to clerks who know very little about such tasks.[45] Consequently, Nigeria's educational system suffers from weak planning and budgeting, poor financial management, and questionable procurement practices.[46]

To incentivize accountability into Nigeria's management system, it is apparent that providing managers with relevant and sufficient data from which to make informed decisions is an important first step. As discussed previously, the absence of data only aggravates the situation by enabling corruption. Additionally, given that the capacity of Nigeria's managers is limited by ignorance as much as malice, future strategies should focus on training as an integral piece of the overall plan. As Hallak and Poisson confirm, "improving transparency in education entails a massive need for training at all levels in the educational system, in particular in the production, analysis, dissemination and understanding of information."[47] Providing quality training is clearly an area in which international organizations can effect positive change and should be an essential element in future accountability strategies.

Ensuring Oversight Integrity

The importance of effective oversight to help incentivize accountability cannot be overstated. According to the Swiss Agency for Development and Cooperation, "Corruption is made possible through a lack of or insufficient supervision."[48] Oversight not only ensures that money is spent for approved purposes, but also that institutions adhere to prescribed financial and administrative regulations.[49] An effective oversight program essentially places a seal of approval on the entire educational system. This sort of "blessing" is important when quality education depends to a large degree on foreign assistance, training, and funding.

In Nigeria, a lack of integrity in the oversight process only worsens the corruption already present in the system. Anastasia Onuorah opines, "The high level of corruption in the public sector of Nigeria is basically as a result of the failure of auditing."[50] Ideally, the oversight process could be handled entirely through mechanisms internal to Nigeria's educational system. However, given the susceptibility of such mechanisms to corruption, the internal auditing process is an unreliable means for enforcing accountability. Therefore, it is essential that internal oversight efforts be combined with independent, external evaluations.[51] These two groups would work with overlapping mandates and serve as compliments to one another.[52] As with management, the international community plays a vital role in oversight by providing the professional, neutral, and independent oversight bodies that are so crucial to maintaining controls and accountability.

It is critical to note that data collection, management, and oversight are dependent on one another for the successful implementation of any one part of the larger strategy. For example, a vigorous data collection system and competent management are essential preconditions for effective oversight.

13

Therefore, success of strategy as a whole is predicated on implementing the three tenets of the strategy in parallel.

IV. Counterargument

An Alternate Approach

It might be argued that, while an indirect approach towards battling corruption has merit, the best way to eliminate corruption is through the direct targeting of corruption itself. A direct approach uses legal and institutional methods to improve the detection, enforcement, and prosecution of corrupt acts that have *already* occurred.[53] The enforcement mechanism of such an approach typically takes the form of watchdog agencies like the Independent Corrupt Practices Commission (ICPC) or some other auditing-type agency designed to root out corrupt practices.[54] Perpetrators of corrupt acts are subject to punitive action that advocates argue have a significant deterrent effect on future corruption. Additionally, the highly visible nature of these punitive cases rouses civil society, providing the necessary political capital for further anti-corruption measures. Finally, advocates reason that a direct approach achieves results that are quicker and more concrete than those of indirect approaches, which can take years to bear fruit.[55]

While this approach might appeal to the average citizen, and often resonates with international audiences, its window of effectiveness is extremely narrow and its success is completely dependent on the country-specific drivers that fuel corruption.[56] In the case of Nigeria, such an approach would fail for the following

14

three reasons. First, as previously mentioned, because corruption is woven into the very fabric of Nigerian society, Nigerians view corruption not as an evil, but as an essential element to everyday life. Thus, overt anti-corruption actions would only serve to polarize much of the population against the implementation of the larger strategy.[57] Second, studies show that direct methods of battling corruption are only effective in countries where governance is high and corruption is low, which is not the case in Nigeria.[58] Finally, in countries like Nigeria, where corruption is widespread, direct methods only get at a symptom of the greater problem. In summary, a direct attack on corruption provides a politically beneficial "quick fix" to the problem and may even achieve early successes. However, over the long-term, its results will likely prove counterproductive and fail to endure.[59]

V. Conclusion

Relevance to U.S. Policy

Nelson Mandela is famously quoted as saying, "Education is the most powerful weapon which you can use to change the world."[60] For Nigeria, corruption of its educational system dulls the blade of this weapon. With corruption undermining efforts to improve education, Nigerians are unable to adequately translate their immense natural resources into national wealth and prosperity. While this problem may seem irrelevant to the United States, Nigeria's failure to achieve universal education for its youth leaves 10 million school-aged children on the street. Lacking education and direction, these children are vulnerable to extremist rhetoric and propaganda from groups such as Boko Haram. This has a natural destabilizing effect on the country that manifests itself in the form of violence, human rights violations, and in the worst cases, terrorism. Therefore, given the U.S.'s ubiquitous need for energy and global commitment to counterterrorism, it is clearly a national interest to see a stable Nigeria in Sub-Saharan Africa. Achieving stability will ultimately depend on how Nigeria tackles the corruption that continues to plague it. While there is no patent solution to this problem, research shows indirect methods of approach best attack the core symptoms that allow corrupt practices to occur. While an indirect approach may take longer and yield less visible results than a more direct approach, ultimately its effects will prove widespread and lasting. Nigeria has 168 million reasons to be hopeful. It's time it invests in this most precious resource.

VI. Recommendations

To better "incentivize accountability" into Nigeria's educational system, this paper offers the following recommendations:

Improving Data Collection

The GoN should reform its accounting system through widespread and mandatory use of computers and other automated systems. This would increase the amount of data in the system and facilitate the auditing process by making it easier to "follow the money trail". With limited computer capacity, it's too easy to falsify documents, lose documents, and slow down the accountability process. Additionally, *the GoN should continue to collaborate with international partners for the use of surveys such as the 2010 Nigeria Education Data Survey.* Surveys are a powerful method for obtaining data about the system. The analysis of that data informs future decision-making and subsequent courses of action.

Strengthening Management Capacity

The GoN should adopt international financial reporting standards (IFRSs) for book-keeping. In addition to standardizing procedures for managers to follow, it would assist in the auditing process because international agencies would have a standardized benchmark from which to conduct the audits. Another area that needs significant attention is the knowledge base of Nigeria's managers. Considering the dearth of qualified managers in its educational system, *the GoN should seek training assistance from International partners for the purposes of upgrading the skill-set of its managers, particularly in the areas of statistics, accounting, and auditing.* As discussed previously, managers implement policy and thus require the necessary skill-set to do so effectively.

Ensuring Oversight Integrity

Due to their susceptibility to corruption, internal auditing agencies are an unreliable source for auditing. Therefore, *the GoN should develop an auditing process that combines both internal and external auditing agencies.* To be effective, external audits must be conducted by a neutral, independent body at random intervals.

U.S. Specific

USAID is the lead U.S. agency for implementation of this strategy. Other nations such as Korea, Japan, the United Kingdom, and France also supply assistance to the GoN along this line of effort, but USAID currently works in parallel with these countries.[61] Therefore, *USAID should strive for better unity of effort with other international partners to develop a common approach toward problem solving in Nigeria.* The military's role in this strategy is extremely limited and its presence could actually be counterproductive.[62] Therefore, *USAFRICOM should maintain a supporting relationship with USAID Nigeria* and be prepared to provide assistance such as infrastructure and logistics support as required.

VII. Notes

[1] "Prepared Remarks of President Barack Obama: Back to School Event," The White House, accessed September 07, 2012, http://www.whitehouse.gov/MediaResources/PreparedSchoolRemarks/.

[2] "Education for All (EFA)," United Nations Educational, Scientific and Cultural Organization, accessed September 19, 2012, http://www.unesco.org/new/en/education/themes/leading-the-international-agenda/education-for-all/.

[3] "Universal Basic Education - Free Primary Education," Universal Basic Education Commission (UBEC), accessed September 07, 2012, http://ubeconline.com/index html.

[4] Jacques Hallak and Muriel Poisson, *Corrupt Schools, Corrupt Universities : What Can Be Done?* (Paris: International Institute for Education Planning, 2007), 21, accessed September 07, 2012, http://unesdoc.unesco.org/images/0015/001502/150259e.pdf.

[5] "Universal Basic Education - Free Primary Education," Universal Basic Education Commission (UBEC), accessed September 07, 2012, http://ubeconline.com/index html.

[6] Bobby Udoh, "Nigeria's Educated: The Biggest Hindrance in Nation-building," *Nation-building Blog* (web log), January 26, 2012, http://bobbyudoh.com/2012/01/26/nigerias-educated-the-biggest-hindrance-in-nation-building/.

[7] Gillian P. Kaduna, "Nigeria's Abandoned Youth: Are They Potential Recruits for Militants?," TimeWorld, February 18, 2012, http://www.time.com/time/world/article/0,8599,2107102,00 html.

[8] U.S. Naval War College, *Joint Operation Planning Process (JOPP) Workbook* (Joint Military Operations Department, Newport, RI: Naval War College, 2012), D-3.

[9] Milan N. Vego, *Joint Operational Warfare: Theory and Practice* (Newport, RI: Naval War College, 2007), PDF, II-3.

[10] Ibid.

[11] U.S. Naval War College, *JOPP Workbook*, D-3.

[12] "Education for All (EFA)," United Nations Educational, Scientific and Cultural Organization, accessed September 19, 2012, http://www.unesco.org/new/en/education/themes/leading-the-international-agenda/education-for-all/.

[13] Emmanuel I. Ejere, "An Examination of Critical Problems Associated with the Implementation of the Universal Basic Education (UBE) Programme in Nigeria," *International Education Studies* 4, no. 1 (February 2011): 1, ProQuest Research Library.

[14] Otive Igbuzor, "The State Of Education In Nigeria," The State Of Education In Nigeria, December 02, 2007, Section 5, accessed October 01, 2012, http://dawodu.com/igbuzor14 htm.

[15] "Nigeria Education Fact Sheet - January 2012," United States Embassy in Nigeria, accessed September 07, 2012, http://photos.state.gov/libraries/nigeria/487468/pdfs/January%20Education%20Fact%20Sheet.pdf.

[16] Ibid.

[17] Ejere, "An Examination of Critical Problems," 3.

[18] "Nigeria Economic Fact Sheet - April 2012," United States Embassy in Nigeria, accessed September 07, 2012, http://photos.state.gov/libraries/nigeria/487468/pdfs/April%20Economic%20Fact%20Sheet%202012.pdf.

[19] "Population below Poverty Line - Country Comparison," Index Mundi, accessed October 15, 2012, http://www.indexmundi.com/g/r.aspx?t=0&v=69&l=en.

[20] "Nigeria Economic Fact Sheet - April 2012," United States Embassy in Nigeria, accessed September 07, 2012, http://photos.state.gov/libraries/nigeria/487468/pdfs/April%20Economic%20Fact%20Sheet%202012.pdf.

[21] Olu Omopariola, "Nigeria's Financial Management Nightmare," National Universities Commission, February 12, 2012, Introduction, accessed October 01, 2012, http://www.nuc.edu.ng/nucsite/File/ILS%202002/ILS-64.pdf.

[22] Thomas Greminger, *Swiss Agency For Development and Cooperation: Combating Corruption Guidelines,* issue brief, September 25, 1998, Introduction, accessed October 15, 2012, http://www.sdc.admin.ch.

[23] Martin Meredith, *The Fate of Africa: From the Hopes of Freedom to the Heart of Despair : A History of Fifty Years of Independence* (New York: Public Affairs, 2005), 182.

[24] Transparency International, *Corruption Perceptions Index 2011,* report, November 2011, accessed October 02, 2012, http://cpi.transparency.org/cpi2011/results/#CountryResults.

[25] Ejere, "An Examination of Critical Problems," 3.

[26] Ibid.

[27] Meredith, *The Fate of Africa,* 181.

[28] Ibid., 180.

[29] "Nigeria's Education System," e-mail message to author, September 28, 2012.

[30] E.o. Iheoma, "Moral Education in Nigeria: Problems and Prospects," *Journal of Moral Education* 14, no. 3 (October 1985): 188, doi:10.1080/0305724850140306.

[31] Anwar Shah and Mark Schacter, "Combating Corruption: Look Before You Leap," *Finance & Development*, December 2004, 6, accessed October 15, 2012, http://www.imf.org/external/pubs/ft/fandd/2004/12/pdf/shah.pdf.

[32] "Accountability," Merriam-Webster, accessed October 15, 2012, http://www merriam-webster.com/dictionary/accountability.

[33] Shah and Schacter, "Look Before You Leap," 3.

[34] "Roslyn, Long Island, NY: The Enron of Education Fraud and Corruption.," ParentAdvocates.org, accessed October 27, 2012, http://www.parentadvocates.org/nicecontent/dsp_printable.cfm?articleid=3546.

[35] National Population Commission (Nigeria) and RTI International, *Nigeria Demographic and Health Survey (DHS) EdData Profile 1990, 2003, and 2008: Education Data for Decision-Making*, report (Washington, DC: National Population Commission and RTI International, 2011), xv, accessed October 15, 2012, https://www.eddataglobal.org/documents/index.cfm?fuseaction=pubDetail&id=329.

[36] Jacques Hallak and Muriel Poisson, *Corrupt schools, corrupt universities: What Can Be Done?* (Paris: International Institute for Education Planning, 2007), 33, accessed September 07, 2012, http://unesdoc.unesco.org/images/0015/001502/150259e.pdf.

[37] Ibid.

[38] Olu Omopariola, "Nigeria's Financial Management Nightmare," National Universities Commission, February 12, 2012, Elements of Accountability, accessed October 01, 2012, http://www.nuc.edu.ng/nucsite/File/ILS%202002/ILS-64.pdf.

[39] Greminger, *Combating Corruption Guidelines,* Establishing transparency.

[40] Hallak & Poisson, *Corrupt schools, corrupt universities,* 34.

[41] Ejere, "An Examination of Critical Problems," 6.

[42] Greminger, *Combating Corruption Guidelines,* Planning and partner assessment.

[43] Omopariola, "Nigeria's Financial Management Nightmare," 3.

[44] Hallak & Poisson, *Corrupt schools, corrupt universities,* 288.

[45] Omopariola, "Nigeria's Financial Management Nightmare," 9.

[46] Ejere, "An Examination of Critical Problems," 3.

[47] Hallak & Poisson, *Corrupt schools, corrupt universities,* 34.

[48] Greminger, *Combating Corruption Guidelines,* Maintaining supervision.

[49] Hallak & Poisson, *Corrupt schools, corrupt universities,* 100.

[50] Anastasia C. Onuorah, "Accountability and Public Sector Financial Management in Nigeria," *Arabian Journal of Business and Management Review (OMAN Chapter)* 1, no. 6 (January 2012): 6, http://arabianjbmr.com/pdfs/OM_VOL_1_(6)/1.pdf.

[51] Hallak & Poisson, *Corrupt schools, corrupt universities,* 99.

[52] Greminger, *Combating Corruption Guidelines,* Maintaining supervision.

[53] Daniel Kaufmann, "Revisiting Anti-Corruption Strategies: Tilt Towards Incentive-Driven Approaches?," in *Corruption & Integrity Improvement Initiatives In Developing Countries* (United Nations Development Program), 63, accessed October 15, 2012, http://mirror.undp.org/magnet/Docs/efa/corruption.htm#4%20Revisiting.

[54] Ejere, "An Examination of Critical Problems," 5.

[55] Kaufmann, "Revisiting Anti-Corruption Strategies," 65.

[56] Shah and Schacter, "Look Before You Leap," 1.

[57] Hallak & Poisson, *Corrupt schools, corrupt universities,* 6.

[58] Shah and Schacter, "Look Before You Leap," 5.

[59] Kaufmann, "Revisiting Anti-Corruption Strategies," 65.

[60] "Education Quotes," Brainy Quote, accessed October 27, 2012, http://www.brainyquote.com/quotes/topics/topic_education.html.

[61] Jill Jupiter-Jones, "USAID: Nigeria's Education System," telephone interview by author, October 12, 2012.

[62] Ibid.

VIII. Bibliography

Abdullahi, Dibal R. "The Causes of Youth Restiveness and Violence in Northern Nigeria." 30-42. Proceedings of The Challenges of Youth Restiveness, Violence and Peace in Northern Nigeria. CLEEN Foundation, 2011. Accessed October 01, 2012. http://www.cleen.org/The%20Challenges%20of%20Youth%20Restiveness%20in%20Northern%20Nigeria%20-%20CIDA.pdf.

"Accountability." Merriam-Webster. Accessed October 15, 2012. http://www.merriam-webster.com/dictionary/accountability.

Ajaja, Patrick O. "School Dropout Pattern Among Senior Secondary Schools in Delta State, Nigeria." *International Education Studies* 5, no. 2 (April 01, 2012): 145-53. doi:10.5539/ies.v5n2p145.

Ajayi, Hannah O. "Early Childhood Education in Nigeria: A Reality or a Mirage?" *Contemporary Issues in Early Childhood* 9, no. 4 (2008): 375-80. doi:10.2304/ciec.2008.9.4.375.

Akindele, Matthew I. "The Challenges Facing Early Childhood Care, Development and Education (ECCDE) in an Era of Universal Basic Education." *Early Childhood Education Journal* 39 (February 12, 2011): 161-67. doi:10.1007/s10643-011-0443-3.

Arong, F. E., and M. A. Ogbadu. "Major Causes of Declining Quality of Education in Nigeria from Administrative Perspective: A Case Study of Dekina Local Government Area." *Canadian Social Science* 6, no. 3 (2010): 183-98. Accessed September 19, 2012. cscanada.net/index.php/css/article/download/j.css...021/1086.

"Basic Education and Gender Equality." UNICEF. September 16, 2011. Accessed September 19, 2012. http://www.unicef.org/education/bege_59826.html.

"Education for All (EFA)." United Nations Educational, Scientific and Cultural Organization. Accessed September 19, 2012. http://www.unesco.org/new/en/education/themes/leading-the-international-agenda/education-for-all/.

"Education Quotes." Brainy Quote. Accessed October 27, 2012. http://www.brainyquote.com/quotes/topics/topic_education.html.

Eigen, Peter. "Message From Transparency International." Introduction to *Corruption & Integrity Improvement Initiatives In Developing Countries*, 1-2. United Nations Development Programme. Accessed October 15, 2012. http://mirror.undp.org/magnet/Docs/efa/corruption.htm#Preface.

Ejere, Emmanuel I. "An Examination of Critical Problems Associated with the Implementation of the Universal Basic Education (UBE) Programme in Nigeria." *International Education Studies* 4, no. 1 (February 2011): 221-29. ProQuest Research Library.

"GDP (purchasing Power Parity) - Country Comparison." Index Mundi. Accessed October 15, 2012. http://www.indexmundi.com/g/r.aspx?t=0&v=65&l=en.

Greminger, Thomas. *Swiss Agency For Development and Cooperation: Combating Corruption Guidelines.* Issue brief. September 25, 1998. Accessed October 15, 2012. http://www.sdc.admin.ch.

Hallak, Jacques, and Muriel Poisson. *Corrupt Schools, Corrupt Universities : What Can Be Done?* Paris: International Institute for Education Planning, 2007. Accessed September 07, 2012. http://unesdoc.unesco.org/images/0015/001502/150259e.pdf.

"HIV/AIDS - Adult Prevalence Rate - Country Comparison." Index Mundi. Accessed October 15, 2012. http://www.indexmundi.com/g/r.aspx?t=0&v=32&l=en.

Source: CIA World Factbook (January 2012)

Igbuzor, Otive. "The State Of Education In Nigeria." The State Of Education In Nigeria. December 02, 2007. Accessed October 01, 2012. http://dawodu.com/igbuzor14.htm.

Iheoma, E.o. "Moral Education in Nigeria: Problems and Prospects." *Journal of Moral Education* 14, no. 3 (October 1985): 183-93. doi:10.1080/0305724850140306.

"Inflation Rate (consumer Prices) - Country Comparison." Index Mundi. Accessed October 15, 2012. http://www.indexmundi.com/g/r.aspx?t=0&v=71&l=en.

Source: CIA World Factbook (January 2012)

Jacob, Ray I. "A Historical Survey of Ethnic Conflict in Nigeria." *Asian Social Science* 8, no. 4 (April 01, 2012): 13-29. doi:10.5539/ass.v8n4p13.

Jupiter-Jones, Jill. "USAID: Nigeria's Education System." Telephone interview by author. October 12, 2012.

Kaduna, Gillian P. "Nigeria's Abandoned Youth: Are They Potential Recruits for Militants?" TimeWorld. February 18, 2012. http://www.time.com/time/world/article/0,8599,2107102,00.html.

Kaufmann, Daniel. "Revisiting Anti-Corruption Strategies: Tilt Towards Incentive-Driven Approaches?" In *Corruption & Integrity Improvement Initiatives In Developing Countries*, 63-82. United Nations Development Program. Accessed October 15, 2012. http://mirror.undp.org/magnet/Docs/efa/corruption.htm#4%20Revisiting.

Kennedy, Odu O. "Strategies In Improving the Policy and Access to Technology Education in Secondary Schools in Nigeria." *International Journal of Academic Research in Business and Social Sciences* 1 (August 2011): 184-92. Accessed October 01, 2012. http://www.hrmars.com/Journals.

"Literacy - Country Comparison." Index Mundi. Accessed October 15, 2012. http://www.indexmundi.com/g/r.aspx?t=0&v=39&l=en.

Source: CIA World Factbook (January 2012)

Meredith, Martin. *The Fate of Africa: From the Hopes of Freedom to the Heart of Despair: A History of Fifty Years of Independence*. New York: Public Affairs, 2005.

Mukhtar, Alhaji L., Mohd A. Ratnawati, and Ahmed T. Shittu. "Girl-Child Education in Northern Nigeria: Problems, Challenges, and Solutions." *Interdisciplinary Journal of Contemporary Research in Business* 2, no. 12 (April 2011): 851-59.

National Population Commission (Nigeria) and RTI International. *Nigeria Demographic and Health Survey (DHS) EdData Profile 1990, 2003, and 2008: Education Data for Decision-Making*. Report. Washington, DC: National Population Commission and RTI International, 2011. Accessed October 15, 2012. https://www.eddataglobal.org/documents/index.cfm?fuseaction=pubDetail&id=329.

"Nigeria Economic Fact Sheet - April 2012." United States Embassy in Nigeria. Accessed September 07, 2012. http://photos.state.gov/libraries/nigeria/487468/pdfs/April%20Economic%20Fact%20Sheet%202012.pdf.

"Nigeria Education Fact Sheet - January 2012." United States Embassy in Nigeria. Accessed September 07, 2012. http://photos.state.gov/libraries/nigeria/487468/pdfs/January%20Education%20Fact%20Sheet.pdf.

"Nigeria Fact Sheet - January 2012." United States Embassy in Nigeria. Accessed September 07, 2012. http://photos.state.gov/libraries/nigeria/487468/pdfs/Nigeria%20overview%20Fac

t%20Sheet.pdf.

"Nigeria Political Fact Sheet - February 2012." United States Embassy in Nigeria. Accessed September 07, 2012. http://photos.state.gov/libraries/nigeria/487468/pdfs/FebruaryPoliticalFactSheet.pdf.

"Nigeria's Education System." E-mail message to author. September 28, 2012.

Odunayo, Wale, and Tola Olujuwon. "Corrupt Practices and Educational Values Attainment in Nigeria Society." *European Journal of Social Sciences* 16, no. 1 (2010): 64-74. Accessed October 01, 2012. http://www.eurojournals.com/ejss_16_1_07.pdf.

Ogboru, I. "Educational Policy and Standards: A Key to a Productive Economy." In *University of Jos*. Proceedings of National Conference on Improving Educational Standards in Nigeria, University of Jos, Jos. 2008. Accessed September 07, 2012. http://dspace.unijos.edu.ng/bitstream/10485/1253/1/EDUCATIONAL%20POLICIES%20IN%20NIGERIA%202008.pdf.

"Oil - Production - Country Comparison." Index Mundi. January 01, 2012. Accessed October 15, 2012. http://www.indexmundi.com/g/r.aspx?t=0&v=88&l=en.

Source: CIA World Factbook

Omopariola, Olu. "Nigeria's Financial Management Nightmare." National Universities Commission. February 12, 2012. Accessed October 01, 2012. http://www.nuc.edu.ng/nucsite/File/ILS%202002/ILS-64.pdf.

Onuorah, Anastasia C. "Accountability and Public Sector Financial Management in Nigeria." *Arabian Journal of Business and Management Review (OMAN Chapter)* 1, no. 6 (January 2012): 1-17. http://arabianjbmr.com/pdfs/OM_VOL_1_(6)/1.pdf.

Oyitso, Mabel, and C. O. Olomukoro. "Enhancing Women's Development through Literacy Education in Nigeria." *Review of European Studies* 4, no. 4 (August 03, 2012): 66-76. Accessed September 19, 2012. doi:10.5539/res.v4n4p66.

"Population - Country Comparison." Index Mundi. Accessed October 15, 2012. http://www.indexmundi.com/g/r.aspx?t=0&v=21&l=en.

Source: CIA World Factbook (January 2012)

"Population below Poverty Line - Country Comparison." Index Mundi. Accessed October 15, 2012. http://www.indexmundi.com/g/r.aspx?t=0&v=69&l=en.

Source: CIA World Factbook (January 2012)

"Prepared Remarks of President Barack Obama: Back to School Event." The White House. Accessed September 07, 2012. http://www.whitehouse.gov/MediaResources/PreparedSchoolRemarks/.

"Roslyn, Long Island, NY: The Enron of Education Fraud and Corruption." ParentAdvocates.org. Accessed October 27, 2012. http://www.parentadvocates.org/nicecontent/dsp_printable.cfm?articleid=3546.

Shah, Anwar, and Mark Schacter. "Combating Corruption: Look Before You Leap." *Finance & Development*, December 2004, 40-43. Accessed October 15, 2012. http://www.imf.org/external/pubs/ft/fandd/2004/12/pdf/shah.pdf.

Simon, Karu. "Youth Restiveness and Violence in Northern Nigeria: A Critical Analysis." 9-29. Proceedings of The Challenges of Youth Restiveness, Violence and Peace in Northern Nigeria. CLEEN Foundation, 2011. Accessed October 01, 2012. http://www.cleen.org/The%20Challenges%20of%20Youth%20Restiveness%20in %20Northern%20Nigeria%20-%20CIDA.pdf.

Sunal, Cynthia S., Dennis W. Sunal, Ruqayyatu Rufai, Ahmed Inuwa, and Mary E. Haas. "Perceptions of Unequal Access to Primary and Secondary Education: Findings from Nigeria." *African Studies Review* 46, no. 1 (April 2003): 93-116. Accessed September 19, 2012. ProQuest Research Library.

Tilak, Jandhyala B. "The Kothari Commission and Financing of Education." *Economic and Political Weekly*, March 10, 2007. Accessed September 07, 2012. http://eledu.net/rrcusrn_data/The%20Kothari%20Commission%20and%20Financ ing%20of%20Education.pdf.

Transparency International. *Corruption Perceptions Index 2011*. Report. November 2011. Accessed October 02, 2012. http://cpi.transparency.org/cpi2011/results/#CountryResults.

Tuemi, Asuka T., and B. N. Igwesi. "Homogeneity of Values and National Integration in Nigeria Education: The Need for Reform." *Asian Social Science* 8, no. 2 (February 2012): 159-63. Accessed September 07, 2012. doi:10.5539/ass.v8n2p159.

Udoh, Bobby. "Nigeria's Educated: The Biggest Hindrance in Nation-building." *Nation-building Blog* (web log), January 26, 2012. http://bobbyudoh.com/2012/01/26/nigerias-educated-the-biggest-hindrance-in-nation-building/.

Udoh, Bobby. "The Problem with the Nigerian Culture." *Nation-building Blog* (web log), March 29, 2011. http://bobbyudoh.com/2011/03/29/the-problem-with-the-nigerian-culture/.

"Universal Basic Education - Free Primary Education." Universal Basic Education Commission (UBEC). Accessed September 07, 2012. http://ubeconline.com/index.html.

U.S. Naval War College. *Joint Operation Planning Process (JOPP) Workbook*. Joint Military Operations Department, Newport, RI: Naval War College, 2012.

"USAID Education Strategy." USAID. February 2011. Accessed September 07, 2012. http://transition.usaid.gov/our_work/education_and_universities/documents/USAID_ED_Strategy_feb2011.pdf.

Vego, Milan N. *Joint Operational Warfare: Theory and Practice*. Newport, RI: Naval War College, 2007. PDF.

Revised edition, 2009